THE ART OF GUIDING

KATRINE PRINCE

With cartoons by
Royston

Continued success!
Jessie ? Rodel

'THE ART OF GUIDING' WAS ORIGINALLY PUBLISHED IN 1997 BY FRONTLINE TOURIST TRAINING LTD

THIS SECOND EDITION IS PUBLISHED BY
The Institute of Tourist Guiding
Coppergate House
16 Brune Street
London E1 7NJ
+44 (0)20 7953 1257
www.itg.org.uk

2ND EDITION © Institute of Tourist Guiding 2008
CARTOONS © Royston Robertson 2008
    www.roystonrobertson.co.uk
All rights reserved

ISBN 978-0-9560762-0-5

DESIGNED AND TYPESET BY
Linda Holmes Graphic Design
lhdesign@btinternet.com

PRINTED AND BOUND BY
Micropress Printers Ltd
27 Norwich Road
Halesworth
Suffolk IP19 8BX
www.micropress.co.uk

CONTENTS

PROLOGUE to the second edition   **5**

1   Setting the Scene   **7**

2   Knowledge   **11**

3   About Personality and the Presentation of Self   **15**

4   Nervousness   **19**

5   About Effective Commentary   **25**

6   About Delivery of Commentary – I   **37**

7   About Delivery of Commentary – II   **47**

8   Questions – their importance and how to handle them   **53**

9   Site, Walk and Moving Vehicle   **57**

EPILOGUE   **71**

PROLOGUE
TO THE SECOND EDITION
OF THE ART OF GUIDING

Since the first edition in 1997 Katrine Prince sadly died. Her family and former business partners Sandra Jack and Ruth Ridgway kindly passed the copyright to the Institute of Tourist Guiding.

Katrine wrote in the original prologue "the seeds of this handbook were sown in the South Pacific, where I was lucky enough to be training tourist guides to interpret their own very special heritage with the help of a local expert. They asked me to leave them with a Guiding Manual". The handbook is the fruit of many harvests.

Katrine Prince

Katrine qualified as a London Registered Blue Badge Tourist Guide in 1974 and within a few years she was a tutor on the London Tourist Board guide training course under Director of Studies Oswald Clark.

By 1984 Katrine had taken over as Director of Studies and she soon consolidated the full integration of the lectures on knowledge with the increasing number of practical sessions on selection and presentation of knowledge. Katrine went on to set

PROLOGUE

up her own company and her comprehensive training skills in guiding and related fields of heritage interpretation were sought throughout the UK and internationally.

In the 1990s Katrine became very involved in FEG (the European Federation of Tourist Guide Associations) providing secretariat and acting as training spokesperson. She was invited to provide training and consultancy in Cyprus, Latvia, Italy, Russia, Switzerland, Malta and, with EU funding, in the Caribbean and the South Pacific.

Katrine was a founder trustee of the Institute of Tourist Guiding in 2002 and was about to become President at the time of her untimely death in 2004. She was at the heart of the Institute's academic committees that set out policy on training both tourist guides and trainers.

It is our great privilege to be able to edit the second edition of this invaluable handbook thus satisfying continuing international demand.

RICHARD SKINNER and **SANDRA JACK**

1

SETTING THE SCENE

'What an attractive person', I thought as I watched a young girl approach our small group gathered in the town square for a walking tour. As she drew closer, her dress simple but spruce, her face broke into a warm smile and she removed her dark glasses as she spoke: 'Good morning! You must be waiting to join me in discovering this small town of ours.'

Introducing herself as Shula, she asked where we were from, how long we had been on the island and how long we were staying. The tour would last about an hour and a half and finish where we were beginning, here in the town square. 'Please be careful crossing our narrow roads; although we have very few motorcars, the cyclists can be quite threatening

1 SETTING THE SCENE

and we drive on the right!'

Drawing a small boy to the front of the group and checking that the Japanese lady at the back understood her English, Shula then pointed to the star-shaped fountain in the centre of the square and explained how this symbolised the recent history of the island. 'We shall now cross the road here and slip down that passageway between the café and the paper shop.' Stopping briefly to take a photograph of the fountain, I caught up with the group as, lost from view, they had reached the end of the passageway and were emerging into a large internal courtyard shaded by an umbrella-shaped tree.

'Let's go and stand in the shade of the tree out of the sun – I would like to tell you about the pale blue house opposite with the small wrought iron balcony.' In fact several houses were pale blue, but only one had a balcony. Positioning ourselves in the welcoming shade so we could see both the house in question and Shula herself, we learned of the general development of the town as she pointed out the architectural influences and the peculiarities that had come about locally. Since the Mayor's office was in the square we also learned about local government structure and how the town's inhabitants lived.

And so the walk continued: I had already crossed the small river that ran through the town centre and noticed a strange object bobbing about in the water. Drawing our attention to it, I was suddenly able to see that in fact it was tethered to the river base, and was a container for a water pollution measure. In the busier main street, anxious that we should have both a good view of the local synagogue and be able to hear her, Shula shepherded us against the wall of a house. Her voice reached us clearly as she spoke more slowly and the wall acted as a sound board for those of us at the back of the group.

SETTING THE SCENE 1

An hour and a half later we found ourselves back in the square, thanked Shula profusely and went off together to the café for a relaxing drink. As I remarked to two of my new found friends a week later, Shula had succeeded not only in giving us the information we had sought, but had opened our eyes to several aspects of the island that had not even occurred to us. What is more, she had bonded us in so short a time into a small group that had continued to enjoy the island together, and for some of whom indeed the friendship might continue after the holiday.

TELL ME, I'LL FORGET
SHOW ME, I MAY REMEMBER
INVOLVE ME, I'LL UNDERSTAND

2

KNOWLEDGE

THE IMPORTANCE OF STRUCTURED LEARNING

In the first instance a visitor takes a guided tour in order to be informed. This is by no means all that guided tour participants seek, although they are unlikely to be consciously aware of other aspects such as enjoying themselves, understanding what they will be looking at and personal care and attention. These aspects and more will be analysed in later chapters. However without a solid foundation of knowledge, no guide can ever be truly professional.

In leading a guided tour, whether around a site, on a walk or over a large area, the professional guide will aim to place

2 KNOWLEDGE

the tour within its wider context as well as bring out the relevant detail. A tour of the local church will no doubt reflect the history of the town or village, but also the architecture and traditions of the country. A walk may well reflect contemporary life and something of the geography or even local geology, whilst a tour further afield will almost certainly bring in national as well as local aspects. More complex knowledge is often required in an art gallery where an artist may be known and displayed worldwide, whereas an international museum with artefacts from other countries requires even more understanding of world cultures generally.

So how do we go about acquiring the necessary knowledge? Most countries where professional guides are trained run lecture series covering all necessary aspects. Where this is not the case, it would be advisable to spend some time reflecting on how to structure such a knowledge base.

In many countries the obvious primary subjects are:

> HISTORY
> ARCHITECTURE

In other countries the following may well be more important:

> GEOGRAPHY and GEOLOGY
> FLORA and FAUNA

All these subjects and many more will be important, but which come first? Having decided on the primary subjects, it is essential to study them systematically providing a firm foundation on which to build. For instance, a walk through an historic city may well require a chronological understanding of how it grew. This will form a framework something like the outside pieces of a jigsaw puzzle. As time goes by a variety of

KNOWLEDGE 2

different types of walk through this city may well be developed, thereby filling in the jigsaw with ever more pieces.

Knowledge must be constantly enhanced, and kept up-to-date as perhaps a building is pulled down and replaced, an old tree disappears or a new statue is erected. The day the last piece is placed in the jigsaw is the day to give up being a guide. The first requirement of a guide is an inquisitive mind and a love of knowledge across the widest range of subjects. The quest to build up knowledge must be never-ending.

Secondary subjects will include many, if not all, of the following:

> PAINTING and SCULPTURE
> THEATRE and MUSIC
> LITERATURE
> RELIGION
> LEGENDS and MYTHOLOGY
> ARCHAEOLOGY
> ECOLOGY

And so on *ad infinitum*.

THE ART OF GUIDING   13

2 KNOWLEDGE

But above all it should not be forgotten that people are ever better travelled and in many instances their top interest is how people live today, what they eat, how they dress, how much they earn, what a house costs, what school system is practised, and so on.

Professional guides must also keep up-to-date with this contemporary information and remain objective in relaying it. Subjective comments may well offend someone within the group.

Having established a firm foundation of wide-ranging knowledge, this will grow by listening to questions asked. Slowly but surely as correct answers are researched, these will be automatically incorporated and used again and again. As we interpret our national heritage for our visitors, each and every one of us plays a part in enhancing international understanding and increasing cross-cultural awareness.

Commentary cannot be learned by heart.

WITHOUT KNOWLEDGE
THE 'ART OF GUIDING' CANNOT BE PRACTISED

3

ABOUT PERSONALITY AND THE PRESENTATION OF SELF

"WHAT AN ATTRACTIVE PERSON!"

The greatest compliment a guide can be paid is that of enthusiasm. The most damning is to be accused of being boring. The professional guide will seek to retain interest by passing on information in an enjoyable and entertaining manner, combining the skills of both the teacher and the entertainer, and thereby develop the specific skills of the art of guiding.

Apart from imparting accurate, objective information the successful guide will:

— have a genuine love of people;

3. ABOUT PERSONALITY AND THE PRESENTATION OF SELF

- have a warm personality and be a 'giver' not a 'taker';

- understand the meaning of hospitality, acting very much as one would host a visitor at home;

- care about the visitor and enquire about special needs and wishes;

- endeavour to meet the needs and wishes of ALL members of the group.

NOTE
WELL BEGUN IS HALF DONE!

The atmosphere for a successful guided tour can be set within the first five minutes of meeting the client, or indeed even less. There may be moments during the tour when an incident causes an initially good atmosphere to weaken and it has to be reconstructed; this will only be possible if the guide has established a positive situation at the opening of the tour. On the whole the visitor is primed for enjoyment although on occasion unhappiness with some other aspect of the tour can make this difficult. This makes it all the more important that the guide aims to win over the client as quickly as possible.

APPEARANCE AND THE 'FEEL-GOOD' FACTOR

How to dress? Undoubtedly this must take different situations into account. Is the way we have dressed:

- suitable for the occasion?

- suitable for the site?

ABOUT PERSONALITY AND THE PRESENTATION OF SELF 3

— suitable for the client?

— comfortable for the duration of the tour?

Confidence in our appearance increases confidence in ourselves, which in turn inspires confidence in our visitors. This is a profession in which first appearances count. Do not dress for the opposite sex! Jealous partners will only make work more difficult.

To wear a tiara when guiding back-packers can be as disastrous as jeans when guiding professional businessmen.

BODY LANGUAGE

Stand tall, not slouching or leaning against a wall or vehicle. Stand and walk freely, with arms swinging naturally. Arms held across the chest is a defensive gesture, whilst hands on hips denote a certain aggression.

SMILE, and above all establish EYE CONTACT. This should be with each and every member of the group, however briefly. Do not fix your gaze on one person only, however sympathetic or attractive – this can be embarrassing for them; but take note of the shy person, the loner, the person walking

THE ART OF GUIDING **17**

3 ABOUT PERSONALITY AND THE PRESERVATION OF SELF

with a stick or the person with the babe-in-arms. This helps bond a group of people and contributes to successful but unobtrusive group management.

Nevertheless be aware of cultural differences: for instance do not impose eye contact on Japanese visitors. Should we shake hands? What do different gestures mean in different cultures and who would disapprove of hands in pockets? In other words, BE AWARE and sensitive to other cultures!

INTRODUCTIONS

Introductions should be made clearly and simply. After a few sentences understanding should be checked, particularly if guiding in English. There are many thousands of different English accents worldwide and each one takes a while to get used to. In addition many non-English speakers will understand English provided it is spoken clearly and distinctly.

4

NERVOUSNESS

It is a well-known fact that actors and professional speakers will often feel nervous or apprehensive before a performance or presentation. Indeed it is said that it is better to feel a little nervous, to experience 'butterflies in the stomach' since the need to overcome these 'butterflies' increases adrenaline flow and thereby energises the system. It is therefore not a bad thing to be nervous. However it is not good to be SEEN to be nervous.

Why are we nervous or apprehensive? We may know there is an expert within the group or indeed the whole group may be experts in some aspect of the tour, such as agriculture

4 NERVOUSNESS

or archaeology. The tour and its unusual itinerary may have been announced at the last moment with too little time to prepare adequately. As a result the following concern us:

— lack of preparation;

— resultant lack of knowledge;

— fear of 'drying up' (a mental block) thereby making ourselves look silly or exposed to ridicule.

This nervousness can show in body language:

— **FEET** may tap or do the 'soft shoe shuffle', constantly moving;

— **HANDS** likewise, knuckles clenched, rings twisted;

— the **BODY** may sway as weight is shifted from side to side;

— **EYE CONTACT** may be avoided;

— but above all the **VOICE** can betray us, wavering, forcing us to swallow as the mouth dries.

FIRSTLY we can consciously take control of the body by:

— adopting a well-balanced stance, fixing feet firmly on the ground and perhaps slightly apart, weight evenly distributed on both hips, spine straight; this will lessen physical tiredness and lends an air of quiet authority;

NERVOUSNESS 4

— **drawing back shoulders** and lodging hands either loosely behind or in a pocket (as custom dictates). This not only improves posture, but also expands the lungs allowing easy intake and exhalation of breath;

— **controlling hands** and considering carefully how they are used: do they wave around uncontrollably and meaninglessly or do they form gestures that are a recognisable extension of what is being said? For instance, when we say: 'Look to the right', do we indicate clearly to the right or is that indication some vague throwaway wave? If we describe an action with our hands as well as with words, we very often help those who are hard of hearing or those who perhaps do not master our language fully;

— **establishing general eye contact** with the entire group or, if necessary, looking just above the eyes between the brows, thereby avoiding too direct a contact, but nevertheless giving the appearance of being aware of each and every one.

SECONDLY, and of fundamental importance, **take control of breathing**.

4 NERVOUSNESS

Not only is this a help in controlling nerves and lessening apprehension, but the voice suffers from incorrect breathing. Simply by taking two or three deep breaths we take control of ourselves. What is more this conscious action deliberately sends more oxygen to the brain.

GOLDEN RULES FOR OVERCOMING A MENTAL BLOCK:

1. **PAUSE** – have the courage to be silent

2. Take that **DEEP BREATH** and send oxygen to the brain, bringing inspiration

3. **WORDS** will flow again

There is never a need to apologise for 'drying up'. Most people will not notice there has been a break in commentary unless their attention is drawn to it. Indeed pauses are positive, allowing for the absorption of knowledge.

Learning just the opening lines of a commentary can act as a 'confidence builder' if nervous about a specific tour. Once launched into delivery, the natural content of the presentation will follow.

TO SUMMARISE

— Look good, feel good!

— S M I L E !

— Establish eye contact;

NERVOUSNESS 4

- Consciously think about well-balanced deportment;
- Develop meaningful hand gestures;
- Practise correct breathing.

ENTHUSIASM + EXPERTISE = CONFIDENCE

ABOUT EFFECTIVE COMMENTARY

AUDIENCE ANALYSIS AND VISITOR EXPECTATION

"SHULA ASKED WHERE WE WERE FROM..."

People take a guided tour to be informed. This information may be extremely in-depth or on the other hand little more than the subtitles for photographs. It is essential therefore to assess the audience correctly. This divides itself into two aspects:

- the people themselves;
- their tour.

ABOUT EFFECTIVE COMMENTARY

FACTORS TO CONSIDER IN ANALYSING AUDIENCE:

- nationality and country of origin;
- age and sex;
- socio-economic grouping and education;
- financial resources;
- special interests;
- how long is their visit?
- have they been here before?
- how much do they already know?
- where else have they been?
- where else are they going?

Some of this information can sometimes be obtained at the time of booking. If this does not apply, an accompanying person such as a tour manager can often supply background information. However the visitors themselves are undoubtedly the best source of information. By allowing time before the tour begins, it is possible to chat and find out a little about the different individuals. Contact can be established by asking a few questions, from which specific interests may well emerge and commentary can be adapted accordingly.

ABOUT EFFECTIVE COMMENTARY

EFFECTIVE COMMENTARY IS TWO-WAY:

(a) Client expectation

It has already been established that a person goes on a tour for information, be it less or more. However, guided tour participants also want to enjoy themselves. The ratio may vary, but both aspects are of equal importance. Information should be delivered in an entertaining manner.

NOTE

INFORMATION SHOULD BE DELIVERED IN AN ENTERTAINING MANNER

In addition, and possibly subconsciously, the participant on the guided tour is also expecting other aspects to the tour.

Be sure to provide what has been promised:

— if specific site visits are on the itinerary, these sites should not be missed;

— if a specific route has been mapped out, it should be followed unless impossible;

— if a time has been set for the end of the tour, keep to it.

Finally, do not forget those small practical snippets of information that keep the visitor happy: how to dial home, how much is a postage stamp and where to buy it, what the local delicacy is and what the most typical souvenir, and finally when, where and how refreshment will be provided.

5 ABOUT EFFECTIVE COMMENTARY

EFFECTIVE COMMENTARY IS TWO-WAY:

(b) Guide intentions

In the role of interpreting local, regional and national heritage there should also be a 'hidden agenda':

PROMOTE home town, home country, the company that has set up the tour and indeed the services of the professional guide – please come back!

DISPEL MISCONCEPTIONS – people travel the world with pre-conceived ideas about a place derived from television and films, maybe from novels and hearsay. Their ideas are sometimes quaint and the aim should be to impart a clearer understanding of the area of interpretation.

INVOLVE the tour participant – a group of visitors that has been successfully involved in the tour is a happy group and its individual members will go away with better memories and greater understanding. To achieve this the professional guide will inspire confidence in the ways discussed, thereby bonding the group together for the duration of the tour.

INFORMATION ENTERTAININGLY DELIVERED

Information is made up of a series of facts or data. Above all data must be accurate. It should also be:

— concise and simple, and therefore easy to understand;

— selective and relevant both to the tour itself and to the client;

ABOUT EFFECTIVE COMMENTARY

- structured and not a simple inventory or list of facts;

- varied, covering all relevant aspects; eg an agricultural tour may well also cover an important building, an interesting geological phenomenon or a day in the life of an agricultural worker;

- above all, objective.

This can be made entertaining and therefore enjoyable by very simple means:

- a smile in the voice as well as the face;

- anecdotes and human stories rather than straight facts;

- positive rather than negative statements;

- humour.

HUMOUR INCREASES LEARNING BY 18-20%

THE ART OF GUIDING

5 ABOUT EFFECTIVE COMMENTARY

Let's consider two of these factors:

Positive Statements

'What a pity it's raining today' is hardly guaranteed to put everyone in a positive frame of mind. Whereas 'The rain will reduce the dust / keep the grass green / make the sun seem even brighter when it comes out' are all positive statements of fact.

A problem sometimes encountered between the itinerant guide on a coach maintaining the tour on a tight schedule and the residential guide on a site occurs when the latter, probably unwittingly and with the best will in world, starts the tour with: 'What a pity you have so little time here. I really shall not be able to show you very much.' Immediately the visitor is dissatisfied, making the tour less easy for both guides involved. How much better: 'I believe you have to be at you next rendezvous in an hour's time; let me show you the highlights of this house.'

Jokes

There are a number of reasons why JOKES should be avoided:

— different nationalities laugh at different things;

— some people are more critical than others about what is funny and what is not funny;

— forgetting the punch line... no, this is not a valid reason, but an amateur reaction: no professional comedian would dream of telling a joke on stage or on screen without rehearsing it, not only down to the punch line, but to the last pause and in every

ABOUT EFFECTIVE COMMENTARY 5

aspect of timing. If a joke has been found to work, use it as a professional, but use it with sensitivity.

Never make a joke at the expense of another and be careful not to offend any individual within a group. Perhaps, after all, it is advisable to avoid jokes!

Beware the PRIMA DONNA! A guide who is too intent on information risks becoming boring, but a guide who is too intent on entertaining risks becoming a prima donna.

PREPARING A SPECIFIC TOUR

Whether on site, on a walk or in a moving vehicle, check in advance:

— ROUTE: are any expected items in the museum temporarily not on view? Is any part of the route blocked off?

— KNOWLEDGE: is it up-to-date? Have previous questions been researched?

— TIMING: has commentary been adapted to the time available?

— CURRENT EVENTS: how could these forcibly modify the tour?

— PAYMENT: who is responsible? Never put personal money up front without first ensuring

5 ABOUT EFFECTIVE COMMENTARY

repayment. Never spend clients' money without authorisation.

— Finally, PLAN B – be flexible, be prepared for any eventuality!

✓ CHECKLIST FOR THE FREELANCE GUIDE

POINTS TO NOTE WHEN ACCEPTING A TOUR

A Who is booking you?

  i. Name
  ii. Address
  iii. Telephone and fax numbers
  iv. Mobile phone number
  v. Email address
  vi. Contact name

B Day, date and time of tour?

C Meeting point with tour and contact name?

D How many in the group?

E If relevant, name of coach company, telephone number and contact name?

F Who is paying any entrance fees?

G Who is paying you?

ABOUT EFFECTIVE COMMENTARY 5

ABOUT STRUCTURING A COMMENTARY

In opening remarks or introduction, include a few aspects of the tour that will grab the imagination of participants; mention a few facts that can be referred to later such as historical links with the home country, an unusual plant, a famous person, a specific artefact. This will give the tour participant something to look forward to and when it is enlarged upon, it will already be familiar.

Slowly developing familiarity with a topic is a simple device to build up understanding; eg what the unusual plant looks like growing, how it is sold in the market place and how it tastes in the restaurant. This technique is also quietly flattering in that, as the theme or topic is developed, tour participants will not feel they are being bombarded with hitherto unknown facts, but are quietly building on acquired knowledge, albeit within a relatively short space of time.

Very early on, bring in the LOOK factor: in other words, point out something VISUAL.

THE 'LOOK' FACTOR

The guide who uses tour participants solely as an audience is not performing professionally as a guide. Guiding is about helping people SEE what they are looking at.

People recall, at the very most, 20% of what they HEAR but recall up to 30% of what they SEE!

People may look at something but, until told what it is, they do not actually SEE it. Professional guiding rectifies this: it

5 ABOUT EFFECTIVE COMMENTARY

helps people SEE what they are looking at.

Only after having established what is VISUAL, introduce a non-visual topic such as the historical fact or the anecdote to clarify a point of information. Try to find a visual trigger even for non-visual information.

This technique is known as
TOP VISUAL PRIORITY

In structuring commentary, try to find links: the person whose statue is in the main square was born in that district, educated at the university, then lived in that country house.

...and back to AUDIENCE ANALYSIS

As the tour progresses, constantly monitor through participant reaction whether or not commentary has been correctly pitched.

If reaction is negative or even absent, modify the commentary accordingly.

Key Question
WOULD I ENJOY MY OWN COMMENTARY?

ABOUT EFFECTIVE COMMENTARY

Here are some useful suggestions for making your commentary more interesting and relevant to your audience, which have now been incorporated into the training of Institute Blue Badge Guides:

TILDEN'S INTERPRETIVE PRINCIPLES (TIPS)

PROVOKE (Beginning)

You must stimulate curiosity, attention and interest in your audience. Ask yourself: why would a visitor want to know this? Start with a provocative question or statement, eg "Why do we collect and preserve these artefacts anyway?"

RELATE (Middle)

Relate the message to the everyday lives of your visitors. Think of examples or comparisons that relate to them. Use lots of analogies to do with size and weight, or food, sex, family, money etc. This is an easy way to incorporate humour.

REVEAL (End)

Aim to reveal the ending through a creative or unusual perspective. The reveal tells the visitor why the message was important for them, or how they can benefit from the information that was interpreted for them.

ADDRESS THE WHOLE

Make sure that your commentary is related to your main theme.

6

ABOUT DELIVERY OF COMMENTARY - I

UNDERSTANDING VOICE

"CLEAR AS A BELL"

A boring voice bores its audience. However, the voice is a remarkable musical instrument which is eminently trainable. It is therefore important to understand how to make the best possible use of voice.

Not only must it not fail – and therefore it needs nurturing – but a voice well-used will enhance our commentary and heighten audience pleasure in listening to us.

6 ABOUT DELIVERY OF COMMENTARY – 1

THE IMPORTANCE OF BREATHING CORRECTLY

Breathing should come from the diaphragm: if we place our hands on the rib cage and we are breathing correctly, we will feel the ribs moving slowly out with every breath inhaled and in again as we exhale.

In order to feel correct breathing, we should lie on the floor in a totally relaxed position. Switching off mentally, we discover that breathing is instinctively lower, deeper and slower.

In order to achieve the same effect while standing, the shoulders should be totally relaxed and the rib cage open. In taking a deep breath (preferably in through the nose and out through the mouth), we must try to re-create the sensation of breathing that was accomplished lying on the floor.

Many of us breathe – at least sporadically – in short shallow intake. This can be caused by temporary nerves, other stresses or lack of assurance. Correcting this improves posture, gives an appearance of confidence and makes it easier to talk for eight hours at a stretch.

A trained actor has speech and breathing exercises three times a week for three years and then would never speak for more than an hour and half to two hours an evening, whereas tourist guides cope with an eight hour working and talking day.

Remember the dictum:

PAUSE take control of your breathing by several long, deep breaths.

Incorrect use of the voice for considerable lengths of time, as in guiding, puts

ABOUT DELIVERY OF COMMENTARY - I   6

unnecessary strain upon the vocal cords. Eventually the vocal cords will no longer operate and the voice will disappear. For this there is no miracle cure, simply REST. In the worst case an operation could be necessary to have nodules removed.

Without a voice, a guide cannot operate. It is therefore well worthwhile to study breathing techniques and if necessary, seek professional help. Many a colleague who has followed a course in breathing therapy has found many aspects improved, not the least that of enhancing voice power.

ABOUT AUDIBILITY

In using voice, our first aim is TO BE HEARD, which is not as foolish a statement as might first appear. If we do not pitch to the outer extremities of the group, individuals will drift away dissatisfied.

RULE

THE VOICE SHOULD BE LOUD ENOUGH!

On the other hand, pitching too far and talking too loudly can also be irritating.

THE ART OF GUIDING **39**

6 ABOUT DELIVERY OF COMMENTARY – 1

POSITIONING TO BE HEARD

We should position both ourselves and our group so that we can be heard. The group should be kept in front of us. We can avoid large numbers standing behind by backing up against as small an object as a thin tree or pole.

In a noisy street it can help to provide a sound board by standing backed against a wall, which will project sound towards the group.

Alternatively, depending on what the group should be LOOKING AT, the people themselves should be shepherded against the wall, the speaker facing it, again allowing the wall to bounce sound back into the group.

Face the group at all times. Remember there may be people who are hard of hearing and are therefore grateful to be able to lip-read to assist their hearing.

Similarly, people whose understanding of English is weak will be helped if they can look at the speaker.

ABOUT DELIVERY OF COMMENTARY – 1   6

On a walk, do not give out information while moving as only those close by will hear.

RULE
NEVER TALK WHILE WALKING

The larger the group, the longer it will take for the speaker's voice to reach those further away. Speak more slowly as well as more loudly.

RULE
THE LARGER THE GROUP, THE MORE SLOWLY ONE SHOULD SPEAK!

RULE
INCREASE VOLUME BY BREATHING CORRECTLY!

To increase volume, be sure to maintain deep breathing and push the volume out on the exhaled breath. Do not rely on vocal cords to increase volume; this will result in shouting and very quickly strain the voice, for which there is no cure but rest.

6 ABOUT DELIVERY OF COMMENTARY – 1

RULE
CLARITY IS AS IMPORTANT AS VOLUME

CLARITY is as important as volume. It is necessary to articulate clearly. Consonants must be crisp and clean; vowel sounds should be as pure as possible. Avoid speaking through clenched teeth – use muscles around the mouth almost as though singing. Practise in front of the mirror mouthing all your vowel sounds and feel those muscles moving – they can almost hurt initially if used properly for the first time.

VARIETY CAN BE ACHIEVED BY CHANGES IN:

P I T C H

vOLUME

SPEED

RULE
SPEED NEEDS PRACTICE!

SPEED needs practice. On the whole it is recommended to speak slowly and clearly. However, speeding up speech will help rouse a sleepy audience or one that has become drowsy from the regular music of the speaker's voice. A few fast sentences can have a surprising effect, but be careful, do not stumble. Practise a few times against a stop watch.

ABOUT DELIVERY OF COMMENTARY – 1   6

EMPHASIS CAN BE ACHIEVED BY:

— Speaking more slowly

— Speaking faster

— Speaking quietly

— SILENCE!

SILENCE is an invaluable tool. It can raise expectations and create suspense in a theatrical manner. But it can also silence others, such as the innocent pair discussing some purchase, oblivious that their chatter is actually disturbing. Try it!

RULE
DO NOT NEGLECT THE VALUE OF SILENCE!

MICROPHONE TECHNIQUE

Modern microphones are very sensitive.

BE AWARE!
Experiment for the best possible microphone reception.

RULE
BE AWARE! EXPERIMENT TO FIND THE BEST RECEPTION

Client reaction to poor microphone is usually to call for the volume to be turned up or down. It is more likely that technique is incorrect.

6 ABOUT DELIVERY OF COMMENTARY – 1

'Pop' stars should not be copied, nor indeed television presenters. Holding the microphone in front of the mouth like an ice-cream cone waiting to be licked is not only unsightly, but inhibits potential lip-reading and muffles the voice, creating feedback into the system which will resonate in the ears of those listening, who will call for the volume to be turned down.

A microphone should be an extension to the face and, depending on type, should be held:

EITHER

on the chin just below the lips in touch with the face so that voice waves pass over the top;

OR

to the side of the mouth in touch with the face so that voice waves flow past it.

If the feel of metal on skin is unpleasant then insert thumb between microphone and face, but in touch with it. This facial contact ensures that voice is not lost when moving the head.

Care should be taken in handling microphones which are delicate instruments. Bus/taxi owners should be encouraged to have microphone leads of a reasonable length to allow the guide to face clients, at least from time to time, with a certain amount of movement.

ABOUT DELIVERY OF COMMENTARY - 1   6

Take care not to sit or stand below an amplifier which leads to feedback through the system.

WORDS AND DATES

KISS!

K-eep

I-t

S-hort

S-imple

KEEP IT SHORT AND SIMPLE is the perfect maxim for the professional guide. Short sentences, simple words. Using erudite words can create a gulf between the guide and the guided.

If a technical word is essential, explain it! The professional guide will be able to make any subject intelligible to the audience and will not make assumptions about knowledge.

When mentioning a PLACE NAME, repeat it slowly, even spell it!

6 ABOUT DELIVERY OF COMMENTARY – 1

DATES should be used sparingly. Certain key dates cannot be omitted, but time can be identified in a number of ways.

> 1 6 7 8
> ... the late seventeenth-century
> ... the late sixteen hundreds
> ... just over three hundred years ago

ALWAYS relate a person to a period. IF POSSIBLE, relate a date to a relevant event in the client country.

NEVER UNDERESTIMATE AUDIENCE INTELLIGENCE !

NEVER OVERESTIMATE PREVIOUS KNOWLEDGE !

46 THE ART OF GUIDING

7

ABOUT DELIVERY OF COMMENTARY - II

UNDERSTANDING THE IMPORTANCE OF THE VISUAL

"DRAWING OUR ATTENTION TO IT..."

In Chapter 5 we talked about **TOP VISUAL PRIORITY**. It will be remembered that people recall a great deal more of what they see than of what they hear. It will also be remembered that the role of the guide is to help people SEE what they are looking at.

7 ABOUT DELIVERY OF COMMENTARY – II

Teachers who spend considerable time making visual aids must envy guides whose visual aids are all around them, the very essence of their work. A guide's visual aids are:

- the artefacts in museums;

- the buildings around us;

- every aspect of the countryside.

The work of a guide is VISUAL. Guiding is not lecturing, but telling people about what they can see. Commentary must be constantly illustrated by what can be seen.

INDICATION

The most obvious way to use the VISUAL is to indicate, to point it out. When indicating, it is important:

- to prepare in advance;

- to indicate in time;

- to hold indication long enough for everyone to see.

> The arm should be fully extended, opening out gracefully from the elbow and held.

> Quickly swinging out half an arm, the elbow close to the body, is useless and looks ridiculous.

ABOUT DELIVERY OF COMMENTARY – II 7

ON SITE – POSITIONING A GROUP TO SEE

NEVER stand in front of what is being described.

This may sound obvious, but it is surprising how often it happens when being taken around by a keen amateur. All too often the enthusiastic amateur seems to find it necessary personally to admire, and thereby block from view, the very object the audience is being asked to admire.

In a museum, stand at the corner of the showcase; in an art gallery, at the side of a painting.

In a church or domestic building when describing a whole room or area, we must think carefully about the best place to position both ourselves and the group to allow all participants to see as much as possible as well as being able to hear.

Think about the size of the group: if it is a large group, talk about items that are visible to the majority of the group, including those at the back. This generally means larger items or aspects that are higher up.
If it is essential to talk about something small either on the ground or at the bottom of a showcase, describe it carefully and then invite those at the back to come forwards to look, giving the necessary time.

Consider the use of GESTURE to extend verbal description: we can also describe the shape of an artefact, the fall of a flower or the position of an effigy with our hands.

7 ABOUT DELIVERY OF COMMENTARY – II

Avoid moving a group unnecessarily. The larger the group, the less it should be moved. The converse is of course true if guiding only a couple of people.

INDICATION ON A COACH OR BUS

NEVER say 'over there' or 'over here'. The response will inevitably be 'WHERE?'

ALWAYS use 'on your right' and 'on your left'.

AVOID the use of 'straight ahead'.

If it essential to talk about something highly visible through the front window, qualify it by adding: 'and shortly on your right/left'. People sitting at the back will not be able to see out of the front window. If they are not told on which side of the coach they will shortly be able to see what is being talked about, they will become

ABOUT DELIVERY OF COMMENTARY – II

dissatisfied and possibly disruptive, breaking down group bonding.

In addition it is seldom enough simply to say 'on the right/left' since there will probably be several buildings/trees/other to choose from. Physical indication must be further qualified by a description. This description can be the colour of what is being indicated, or its shape, or its exact position, such as 'the house on the left with the red door', 'the octagonal building to the right' or 'the tree by the roadside on the left with the yellow flowers'.

QUESTIONS
THEIR IMPORTANCE AND HOW TO HANDLE THEM

"SHULA'S MANNER INVITED QUESTIONS"

Questions tell us:

- that the client is listening and interested, giving further clues about special interests;
- that we are approachable and the information we give out is accepted;

8 QUESTIONS

- that we are successfully involving the client in the tour.

However, questions can be an irritant when:

- they interrupt, are irrelevant or pre-empt us;
- the questioner is showing off;
- they are provocative or even rude;
- we cannot answer them!

THE CORRECT TECHNIQUE FOR ANSWERING A QUESTION

First and foremost, SHOW PLEASURE;

LISTEN properly and let the speaker finish. (How often do we think we know the question, answer it quickly, only to find it is not quite the right answer to the right question?).

Then, REPEAT THE QUESTION.

WHY REPEAT THE QUESTION?

- To INVOLVE the group

If we answer only the questioner, even embark on a conversation, we shall lose the remainder of the group who have perhaps not heard the question. Others will feel left out even though they may well also be interested. This is the danger in speaking to those at the front of the coach; similarly in a museum, failure to include the whole group will result in an increasingly diminished group;

QUESTIONS 8

— to be sure we UNDERSTAND;

— to give ourselves TIME FOR THE ANSWER.

Only **now**, give the answer! And in giving the answer remember the maxim **K I S S** – be concise! Too lengthy an answer could lead to a secondary commentary.

HANDLING DIFFICULT QUESTIONS

To avoid the question that interrupts, is irrelevant or pre-empts, fix a time for questions in advance.

By correctly repeating a question, the show-off or silly question is in itself shown up. More often than not, others in the group will spontaneously provide the answer and thereby themselves solve the problem of this difficult client.

Provocative, personal or offensive questions should be politely side-stepped.

And finally, if we do not know the answer to a question, above all, NEVER LIE!

There may be someone within the group who does know the answer. By inventing an answer, we risk destroying our entire credibility.

NOTE
NEVER LIE !

Sometimes, by the mere fact of repeating the question, we realise that we may have an idea; we can answer accordingly.

THE ART OF GUIDING

QUESTIONS

We can offer to find out or indicate where the client can find the answer.

In handling both difficult questions and difficult clients, NEVER be rude, get angry, put a person down in front of others;

This only aggravates the situation. Nor is it necessary to panic. Keep cool and calm.

DISARM WITH CHARM!

9

SITE, WALK AND MOVING VEHICLE

SITE GUIDING

To some extent the guidelines are the same whether in a museum, a religious building or a secular building. First and foremost it is essential to liaise with the person in charge to ensure that all house-rules are observed. Check – in the case of outsiders – that guiding is allowed and follow any regulations that may be in force, such as a particular route, room closures, maximum numbers, guiding in the same room as another guide, and so on.

9 SITE, WALK & MOVING VEHICLE

Be sure to give the group any relevant instructions or information in advance, such as that artefacts in a museum should not be touched, whether photography is allowed; in a church men should remove their hats, in a synagogue men should cover their heads; in a mosque shoes should be removed, and so on.

Once on the site **GROUP CONTROL** should be practised:

— make sure the whole group can **see** what is being described;

— make sure the whole group can **hear**;

— make sure the group is positioned in such a way as to **allow other visitors to pass** and if the group grows, as often happens, interrupt the commentary to repeat the requirement to allow free flow to other visitors;

— when moving through a building, be sure to give **advance instructions** such as steps, low beams or other **hazards**;

— before moving on, give some indication of where the group will **next stop** to allow for individuals who are lingering to look more closely at something that has their special attention to catch up.

MUSEUMS AND ART GALLERIES

Such sites do not always have a thread that can be followed throughout the tour. A succinct introduction is therefore essential to provide 'hooks' on which to hang later information:

SITE, WALK & MOVING VEHICLE 9

maybe the founder's intentions or the growth of the collection.

Positioning within a single room or gallery is very important, to maximise what can be seen. A freestanding glass case sometimes allows people to collect around it without impeding sound and therefore hearing the guide. However, the guide can usually stand at one corner of even a long series of cases and, provided very clear verbal indication is given of where each item mentioned can be seen, it is not necessary for the guide to draw nearer to the said item.

Think very carefully about POSITIONING.

Minimum movement, maximum viewing.

Remember! The larger the group, the larger and higher the item.

RULE
THINK CAREFULLY ABOUT POSITIONING

RELIGIOUS BUILDINGS

Observe the ritual of the building in question. It is essential to understand the religion about which we are speaking and then to include within the introduction a simple explanation.

RULE
OBSERVE THE RITUAL!

For instance the Jewish faith does not bury its dead within the building as Christians very often do; in some cases women worship separately from men. Where is the sacred area? What is sacred about certain rituals?

9 SITE, WALK & MOVING VEHICLE

Never take religious beliefs of a group for granted: for instance a group of Arabs, assumed to be Moslem, may include some Coptic Christians; or vice versa. A group of apparent Anglicans may include some Moslems. Do not assume all Japanese know about Shintoism or all Chinese Confucius. Even those who in the past practised cannibalism incorporated beliefs and rituals which were contravened at one's peril. Never mock, never joke.

Within commentary therefore incorporate respect for any aspect that should be observed whilst within the building: moments of prayer, silence, not walking over certain spots, and so on.

Do not treat a religious building purely as a secular site.

SECULAR BUILDINGS

Seek a theme to the site as a thread for commentary.

These include castles, stately homes, homes of famous people, where there is usually a strong basic theme. That theme should be followed from room to room and developed with informed background knowledge, be it the lives

SITE, WALK & MOVING VEHICLE 9

of the people who lived there, the role of the architect, the style of furniture or indeed its situation in a park, on an island, with a view.

Avoid too much emphasis on detail at the expense of the framework; in other words always make an effort to set detailed information into the background theme story. This can be difficult if covering one room only, and is a problem that should be addressed throughout the team of guides working within such a building.

LEADING A GUIDED WALK

All the techniques employed on SITE should be practised on a walk, such as group management and positioning.

Positioning to be heard: voice projection needs particular care in the open air. Even wind can blow sound away. So we must think about where we stand: allow the wind to carry it if necessary! Remember, where possible, to use a wall as a sound board.

In a town it is more important than ever to ensure that no paths are blocked, particularly where local citizens are going about their daily business. Give thought to where roads should be crossed. Remind clients of the rules of the road, pointing out from which direction traffic is to be expected.

However, do NOT take responsibility for seeing all clients across the road: it is sufficient for one person to have dallied over a photograph and then to rush forwards to catch up with the group and step in the path of a car for the whole tour to be destroyed in a tragedy. Encourage all members of

9 SITE, WALK & MOVING VEHICLE

a walking tour to take personal responsibility for their own safety.

In the countryside, give advance warning about hazards such as uneven ground, poisonous plants, dangerous insects, etc.

RULES

DO:

- think about positioning;
- think about local citizens;
- give advice on safety.

DO NOT:

- take responsibility for the safety of others.

SITE, WALK & MOVING VEHICLE 9

GUIDING 'ON THE MOVE'

COACH, BUS, TAXI OR BOAT

The major difference 'on the move' is that the guide is no longer able to control TIMING. Vehicles move and are controlled by other traffic features (or in the case of boats also by tides, waves and mooring facilities). The guide's commentary must therefore be adapted to outside factors and take these into account.

First and foremost, check the number of clients in the group and re-count after any stop. Do not rely on others or make a summary guess. Leaving one person behind at an isolated spot could have disastrous consequences.

The importance of POSITIONING falls away to be replaced by remembering the POSITION OF THE CLIENT IN THE VEHICLE.

Remember that the guide in the front usually has the best view, the widest vision. Some member of the group will have the worst, perhaps tucked in the back of the vehicle. That client has as much right to the guide's attention and forethought as the client sitting right close to the guide. Remember that each has paid the same fee for the guide's services.

The most important aspect of this is INDICATION:

— do not indicate solely for those in front, viz. 'in front of you';

— remember those at the back who cannot see forwards;

— 'In front' – if absolutely essential – and 'shortly on your right/left'.

9 SITE, WALK & MOVING VEHICLE

Make sure the commentary is timed early enough for all to see what is being indicated. It is better to be too early, provided clear indication is subsequently made at the right time. Never talk about something that has been passed: if already passed by, leave it out. Indicating 'we have just passed...' only leads to irritation on the part of clients that they have missed something.

Think about INDICATION: point out an object if possible; add verbal indication to 'on the right' or 'to the left' such as the green door, the trees with the mauve flowers, the triangular mountain, the boat with the billowing sail. If something ahead is very obvious, which can be seen by those in front but not by those at the back, add: '…and shortly on the left/right' (as will be the case, since the vehicle is unlikely to drive straight into it!).

Specify: if pointing out a specific tree amongst many, describe the form of the tree, the shape of the leaf, the colour of the blossom or its proximity to something else more reasonably recognisable. If pointing out a house amongst many, describe the colour, the shape of the windows or some other identifying feature.

Do not talk privately to those closest, who are likely to be full of questions. If the question is of general interest, repeat it – even over the microphone if necessary – and give a general answer, possibly incorporated into the overall commentary. If the question is specific to the client, postpone further discussion until a natural break.

CAR-GUIDING
The totally personal touch!

Guiding either a chauffeur or self-drive requires a much more conversational approach since there will very often be only a couple of clients. Positioning is easier, group management negligible, and client interests to be catered for in the closest detail. The client may be very demanding of knowledge or alternatively happier talking about himself. This is one-to-one service.

THE COMPLEX TOUR
Many tours are a combination of coach, walk and site. Commentary should be thought through in advance to link specific angles of common interest. If travelling to an agricultural site, commentary will be different from that travelling to a prehistoric religious site.

9 SITE, WALK & MOVING VEHICLE

RULE: ADAPT TO NOT BEING IN CONTROL OF TIMING!

Adapt to no longer being in control of timing.

Be sure to know numbers within the group: leaving a client behind causes problems.

Remember: the client at the back is as important as the client in front.

Remember:

— indicate for the client at the back.

— timing is all important – forget what is passed.

— indicate both physically and verbally.

Here all the skills of the professional guide come into play: not only the practical skills of site-guiding, walks and guiding on the move, but the ability to link commentary together to bring all aspects together and meet every demand for the successful tour.

SELF-ASSESSMENT

The work of the tourist guide is one that can offer enormous job satisfaction. The majority of clients are ready to enjoy themselves. They do not set out to complain. However, if the guide is not professional, has not prepared, and does not practise professional techniques for the benefit of EVERY client within a group, a client may well simply leave the tour. Alternatively there will be complaints. We as guides are only as successful as each and every separate tour.

SITE, WALK & MOVING VEHICLE 9

On the other hand, we should not allow the easy praise that comes from the client who has had an enjoyable time to give a false impression of success. We should occasionally take the time to reflect on whether we would have enjoyed our own tour.

Above all, we should not be persuaded into believing that large tips are the sign of success.

Some cultures tip, others do not. Some people will be reluctant to tip if the person in front has not done so. Others may consider us too 'well-informed' to 'insult' us by tipping. A professional guide does not solicit tips. A tip is a welcome bonus and if working with a driver, to be shared 50/50.

FIRST AID and INSURANCE

All professional guides should follow a First Aid course, however brief. There is as much to learn about what NOT to do, as what to do.

All accidents, however minor, should be reported to the

9 SITE, WALK & MOVING VEHICLE

tour organiser.

All guides should be covered for Public Liability, either independently or through the employer, where relevant. Public Liability Insurance is cover in the event of a client suing for damages.

If personally driving a client, it is essential to have Private Hire insurance. Ordinary car insurance is not sufficient. In the event of an accident there could be claims which will run into the millions.

IN CONCLUSION

In summary, guiding is about communication and public relations. As guides we are communicators, be it a few or too many. Our aim is therefore to be more effective speakers with a view to:

— retaining interest;

— making tours both informative and enjoyable.

It is therefore in our own interest to:

— develop our own style in accordance with our respective personalities;

— above all, ENJOY ourselves and communicate ENTHUSIASM!

SITE, WALK & MOVING VEHICLE 9

**TELL ME, I'LL FORGET
SHOW ME, I MAY REMEMBER
INVOLVE ME, I'LL UNDERSTAND**

EPILOGUE

You have now read nine chapters on *The Art of Guiding*. But beware! Could you learn to dance simply by watching Nureyev? Could you learn to sing by listening to Pavorotti? Can you learn to guide by reading this handbook or indeed by imitating others?

The Art of Guiding must be both taught and practised. The UK format covers a trainee-period of at least one academic year assimilating knowledge and at the same time practising the techniques of selection and presentation. Not only do we teach trainees, but we also train trainers how to teach this skill.

This has been recognised worldwide and is now enshrined in FEG's *The Way Forward* and in CEN standard 15565:2007 *Requirements for the provision of tourist guide training and qualification programmes*.

The Art of Guiding represents a true profession, which is in part information ('the teacher') and in part performing ('the entertainer'). Knowledge is not too difficult to acquire, since most of us are inspired by the love of our own heritage. However, how to impart this enthusiasm is not as simple as it at first may seem. Do not ignore the benefits of professional training in the Art of Guiding.

The Institute of Tourist Guiding and FEG offer teams of highly competent professional trainers, ready to share in many languages the Art of Guiding.

London August 2008